NEWBORN SLEEP FOUNDATIONS

A HANDY GUIDE FOR THE FIRST 16 WEEKS

GEMMA COE,
CHILD SLEEP SPECIALIST

Newborn Sleep Foundations:
A Handy Guide for the First 16 Weeks

ISBN: 978-2-7224-1879-0

The information provided in this book is intended for general guidance and advice only. It is not a substitute for professional medical advice, diagnosis, or treatment. Always seek the advice of your doctor or other qualified health provider with any questions you may have about your child. The author and publisher deny any liability for any direct, indirect, or consequential loss or damage incurred by any individual in connection with the use of this book or its contents.

For Élodie and Charlie

CONTENTS

WELCOME!

On your little one's behalf, thank you for caring and putting time and energy into learning how to meet their sleep needs.

This book was born from the desire to make my popular 'First Steps' package more accessible to new parents. First Steps aims to support new parents with sleep in the early days. We're not touching on sleep training at all, just establishing some healthy foundations and covering all the basics.

Those signing up for First Steps often tell me they just want an opportunity to ask lots of questions or want to do things right from the start. Often, they've been poor sleepers themselves or shift workers and need to prioritise sleep for overall family health and wellbeing. If this sounds like you, then you're in the right place!

This guide brings all the information from the First Steps package into a comprehensive guide for the first 16 weeks. You can read from cover to cover, or simply dip in and out of the chapters that matter to you now.

In this guide, we're going to take a holistic look at children's sleep. That's all the pieces of the jigsaw puzzle; the sleep environment, routine (or just how long a baby has been awake if they're a newborn), and how the baby falls asleep in addition to how much sleep they are getting.

We will be mindful of the whole family and how they are bearing up, including siblings, work pressures, feeding struggles, developmental progress and other things.

This is **NOT** designed to be a book about sleep training your child. It's designed to be a book about navigating the first steps, setting the sleep foundations, and understanding the principles of how to create a happy, healthy sleep set-up for your new baby.

If you feel more structured sleep training is the next step (when your baby is older) then there are a multitude of ways to support this process. The term is often associated with just one or two cry-based methods which certainly don't suit all. The 'sleep space' online can feel cluttered and full of opinions, many of which are unwelcome! If the time comes when you'd like to consider sleep training, try not to be influenced by other people's thoughts and ideas. There will be a good fit for your family, parenting style, and your baby's temperament.

Please do reach out to find a personalised approach for your family.

About the Author

Gemma Coe is an award-winning, certified baby and child sleep specialist, as well as a teacher, author, and mum of two. As a child sleep consultant, she assists families around the world in preparing for their little one's arrival, establishing healthy sleep habits, and providing support for any sleep-related concerns.

Gemma has had a successful career in medical education, healthcare, and teaching. She retrained as a child sleep specialist after navigating her own daughter's sleep challenges. Currently, she works as a sleep expert for both Huckleberry and Ergobaby.

Gemma's approach focuses on the biological and psychological aspects of sleep, employing personalised, evidence-based, and holistic methods to enhance the wellbeing of the entire family.

@childsleepspecialist

www.childsleepspecialist.co.uk

CHAPTER 1
BABY SLEEP FOUNDATIONS

Before we start, I want to assure you, that yes, we absolutely can work on newborn sleep. However, let's not confuse this proactive approach with structured and (often) rather strict sleep training methods.

For me, the definition of 'sleep training' means working on sleep. When we work on sleep, we look holistically at both day and night sleep.

So yes! We can introduce some gentle, thought-through strategies to help our little one's sleep. Think more about 'healthy sleep habits' or 'setting sleep foundations' rather than using a strict sleep training method here though.

Sadly, I can't guarantee you a good night's sleep with a new baby… so we can perhaps cross off the 'sleep through the night' goal on your checklist. Sorry.

However, I can help to start you down the path of helping your baby to fall asleep and stay asleep over the longer term.

They're brand new! What do I need to know?

What do you want to achieve? We need to set age-appropriate goals. The following is considered NORMAL for newborn sleep:

- Multiple night wakings
- Multiple night feeds
- Multiple naps
- Highly variable nap lengths (ten minutes to three hours)
- Late 'bedtime'.

So, if you're set on your baby sleeping through the night, then I'm afraid you're not going to find those answers here. (If I had them, I would be very rich!)

On a side note, some babies just do sleep through the night, and good for them. Please don't compare yourself to other families from your pre-natal group or friends. Every baby is so different.

We'll continue to focus on what we can control, eg bedtime routines, introducing healthy sleeping habits, and slowly shifting bedtime earlier.

We might also be able to look at using a gentle sleep training method to see if we can help babies to fall asleep in more than just one way. This can be helpful for a few reasons.

In the early days, it's often helpful to have a range of methods that support your baby to fall asleep, for example, rocking, feeding, patting, walking, or in a pram. Some babies will also be happy in their cot with just a heavy hand or sensing you nearby. Having multiple ways of falling asleep can help prevent strong sleep associations with just one method (eg feeding or rocking) further down the line.

When your baby can fall asleep in multiple ways, you can start sleep training when they're a little older by slowly reducing the amount of time you use a method that involves a lot of help, eg gradually feeding to sleep less, then rocking less, then patting less. They do a little more, and you do a little less. Gradually, over time. They probably won't notice.

Why is sleep important for babies?

Sleep is vital for EVERY system in our body!

Infant sleep is also known as 'polyphasic'. Lots of phases with lots of wakings. This is entirely normal. Only really by the time your baby reaches three or four months of age do we start to see more of a 'pattern' appearing with distinct sleep periods.

When they reach three (ish) years of age their bodies will become 'monophasic' like adults. One period awake followed by one period asleep.

Did you know... Until your child is about three years of age, they're likely to spend more time sleeping than awake!

Sleep is the absolute foundation of good health, and for children, good development. Working on sleep can mean making tiny, but positive changes. Even small steps in the right direction will turn your little one into a strong and independent sleeper when they're ready.

How to establish a bedtime routine

I bang on about a good bedtime routine quite a bit. Even at a young age, it helps to make a slow, steady, (and importantly) predictable transition between day and night. Going from a room full of friends and family to being put down in a cot and expected to sleep is going from hero to zero!

Just like adults, we need a short period to unwind, slow our heart rate and breathing, and get comfy before falling asleep.

Whilst you don't have to bathe your baby every night, you may want to consider a wash, pop on some lullabies, feed, change their nappy, change into a clean sleep suit and swaddle/sleeping bag, and then begin to support them to fall asleep.

It helps to move into a dimly lit room for the last part of the routine, slowly shutting off the sights and sounds of the environment and removing all the noises and stimulation.

A consistent bedtime routine will stay with your baby throughout their childhood. Think about your adult bedtime routine, I bet that's been the same for years!!

Introducing environmental sleep cues

For me, my sleepy cue is my pillow. When my head hits it, that's it, I'm closing my eyes, and my body understands what's next. If someone removed my pillow, I'd be pretty cross and would have a really hard time falling asleep. It's also why babies get pretty cross when we remove their sleep crutches like feeding or rocking them to sleep!

For our babies, sleepy cues can be a particular nursery rhyme, the sound of the white noise being turned on, the sleeping bag, parent shushing, a baby massage, or some back or bottom pats. Feeding and rocking are the most common cues in the early stages.

What you say to them is equally important, especially as these words will probably stay with your little one until they are a much older child. It can be 'night night little one, love you, sleep tight.' Whatever feels right to you.

After a few nights of working on introducing some easy but predictable baby sleep cues, they will start to feel familiar to the whole family. The bedtime routine becomes more of a bedtime ritual. Humans are creatures of habit!

Predictability also brings comfort.

Using music to aid the transition between day and night

There's certainly a reason why nursery rhymes stick around! They've been tried and tested over many generations and have stood the test of time for a reason.

Typically, they have quite rhythmic and predictable melodies that promote a sense of calm. Researchers at Harvard Music

Lab (1) found that lullabies helped calm and improve babies' sleep. They found it can even lower heart rates and dilated pupils.

Another study (2) on music therapy with premature infants (in a NICU setting) showed playing music helped with their heart rate, respiratory rates, and stress levels. Calm and relaxed babies are well-primed for good-quality sleep.

Many parents like to use one or more of the following to create a nice peaceful and soothing sleep set-up:

- Singing lullabies
- Lullabies playlists (streamed via apps like Spotify)
- Classical music
- Heartbeat/womb noises
- White noise machines.

Whether you choose to play lullabies or soft music on a device, are happy singing to your baby, or are using white noise, they can all be integrated as an important part of your baby's bedtime routine and help them to fall asleep quicker.

The music may not 'send' them to sleep, but it certainly helps to create a nice environment in which they can switch off and they've essentially been prepped for baby sleep time.

What's best: music, lullabies or white noise?

As a sleep specialist, I'm a huge fan of white noise. It has consistency, which is pretty much my favourite thing ever!

White noise acts as a constant in the room and can also help drown out other noises such as those in the household (doors slamming, noisy siblings) and those in the environment (cars outside, birds tweeting, thunderstorms).

It helps set the scene where your baby falls asleep in the same environment that they will wake up in at night as it is the same sound all night long. So, my preference would be white noise during the night and for a nap. Parents singing lullabies will only ever be present at bedtime, not all night long.

Lullabies are great for scene setting and calming and soothing a fussy baby. You can listen to lullabies as part of the bedtime routine and then switch over to your white noise machine when you're popping them down to fall asleep.

Safe volume

Thinking about a 'safe' volume, the American Academy of Pediatrics (3) suggest we wouldn't want the sound to exceed 50dB and you should also place the machine across the room from your baby. For a point of reference, 50–60 dB is about the same level as an adult conversation.

Dial up the calm (for you both)

Remember, emotions transfer! It's hard to stay calm and content when someone next to you is upset, worried, anxious or frustrated.

A calm, peaceful parent singing soft and gentle lullabies to their baby will certainly help promote a sense of calm and relaxation for children. The very set-up we need to relax into better sleep.

What are baby sleep cues?

It's really tricky to work out what your baby is thinking or requires! With sleep cues, some babies will have obvious signs of tiredness such as yawning or rubbing their eyes. Other babies' cues will be missed if you turn your back for a second!

Understanding your own baby's cues will take time and patience. However, this is worth doing. If we can spot their early tired signs, then it allows us to start a simple naptime routine and get them down to sleep at the 'optimal' time. We can help avoid overtiredness, which can make it tricky to settle our baby.

Early sleepy cues to watch for:

- Your baby slows
- Sudden disinterest in their toy or stares into space
- Yawning
- Heavy eyes
- Red eyebrows
- Feeding is less active

Late sleep cues/overtiredness:

- Upset, hard crying
- Very fussy/fractious/irritable
- Arches away/won't be held
- Rubs eyes

Craft a simple daytime routine

I'll be honest with you. Yes, the idea of a 'routine' or 'sleep schedule' with a newborn can feel a little daunting, or even impossible. They sleep (often), they eat (often), and they look around in awe and curiosity, then they sleep again!

Hence, the only newborn routine I could ever recommend is just that: Eat, Play, Sleep. I'm not going to explain each step, they're rather self-explanatory.

Following a simple structure like Eat, Play, Sleep does have a few advantages:

1) Most humans like some sort of structure and definition to their day. It helps with expectation management and transitions. If this is your first baby, then transitioning from a daily work routine to life with a newborn can throw you. So even getting a little structure back can help things feel more 'normal' amidst the newborn chaos.

2) This helps to structure feeds too. If using Eat, Play, Sleep, your baby will be fed after their nap, rather than before it. Usually, this means that the baby will be more awake, taking a good feed until they're full and not falling asleep whilst being fed (breast/chest/bottle). We can then help the baby learn lots of other ways to fall asleep, not just feeding to sleep.

TOP TIP! You may want to dedicate some of the playtime to being in the baby's room whilst awake. Whether that's the room you share at the moment or their eventual nursery. This helps to develop a sense of familiarity (and safety) within their sleeping space.

Take opportunities that exist!

In the first 12–16 weeks, most of the time, your little one will fall asleep on you. Contact naps are pretty frequent at this age and absolutely PLEASE enjoy those newborn snuggles for as long as you can (before they grow old enough to start poking you in the face and pulling at your lips).

If your little one is calm, has had a nice feed and change and it's getting close to their naptime then why not try and put your baby in their cot or side sleeper? You can always lie next to them so they are reassured by your presence. If they remain happy just see what happens.

You never know, given the opportunity, they may just drift off. If so, celebrate. (Or take the opportunity for a much-needed shower, cup of tea, or a nap yourself!)

If they don't drift off and fall asleep then that's fine too. It has still provided a great learning experience and an opportunity to become really familiar and happy with their own sleep space.

Try to put your baby down again the next day. Each opportunity will feel that little bit more familiar and at some point, over the next week or so, they may just start to fall asleep independently or with minimal input such as a gentle touch or your voice to soothe.

Consider wake windows (rather than a 'by the clock' schedule)

You won't find any strict schedules here.

I actively try to dissuade my clients with young babies from aiming for a strict 'by the clock' schedule.

Newborn sleep is so variable, they may nap for just ten minutes, or three or more hours. You can feel like you're chasing your tail with a written schedule, so here's where wake windows come in.

- You can expect a newborn to be awake for about 30 minutes.
- One month: between 45–90 minutes.
- Two months: between 1.25–1.75 hours.
- Three months: between 1.25–2 hours.

Keeping an eye on how long your baby has been awake helps you settle them back down for their next nap when they're more naturally ready for their next sleep. It can help prevent situations where you're trying to settle them when they're overtired or under tired and when falling asleep is much harder.

Remember wake windows are a useful guide, and as every baby is different, you may find your child has slightly longer or shorter wake windows.

Watch and wait!

Newborn sleep is admittedly a little weird. They can make some funny faces!

Newborns will transition between just two sleep stages. Active sleep and quiet sleep. They don't have the distinct sleep stages of an adult – this development occurs at the (sometimes dreaded) four-month sleep regression.

During active sleep, they can look quite strange! All sorts of amazing facial expressions can occur. Also, they can shimmy, shuffle, and even look like they're awake when they're not.

If your newborn is awake in the middle of the night and having a little whinge, whine, moan, groan or other low-level noise, then take a minute or two to stand back and hold off. See what happens. If they wake up fully and start to cry loudly, for sure, get them up, check their nappy, and offer a feed if needed. But otherwise, try not to rush and step in straight away.

Allowing them awake time in their sleep space helps them to familiarise themselves with that environment. If they are happy, then spending some time there is great – hey, you may even be able to shower!

At nighttime, it also offers the opportunity for them to fall back to sleep unaided. Even if it's just once a week!

TOP TIP! You may want to dedicate some daily playtime in the baby's room whilst awake, whether that's the room you share now or their eventual nursery. This helps to develop a sense of familiarity and safety within their sleep space.

Chapter 2

Setting Sleep Foundations vs Sleep Training

When will my baby sleep through the night?

This has absolutely no set answer at all. There are so many variables at play that it is impossible to predict!

Honestly, we're playing the long game. There is no newborn sleep training technique that you can use where you can put your baby down and they stay asleep until morning!

On a side note, some newborn babies do sleep through the night, although most babies certainly do not – some lucky parents out there, eh?

So, what can we do? We can take the opportunities that present themselves and accept that everything we do is just an opportunity to practice. We also need to try and stay cool, calm, and confident when it's all going wrong. (I appreciate that's easier said than done!)

Alongside this list of important things to do, make sure you're following all the recommended sleep environment and SIDS guidelines. Focusing your efforts on these things will help set your little one up to be a fabulous sleeper.

When can I use a more structured sleep training method?

Many parents tend to start thinking about a gentle sleep training method or using other approaches such as controlled crying closer to the six-month mark when you can expect a little more structure to days and nights.

Methods are ultimately aiming to help teach independent sleep skills and how to self-soothe – this can be done with a variety of sleep training techniques. Some are designed to be slow and progressive, over several weeks or months, and typically these methods aim to minimise crying. Other approaches aim to speed up the process of helping your child to fall asleep independently. Typically, the parent will be outside the room and tend to their child at intervals.

Gentle sleep training methods such as the 'chair method' or 'habit stacking' can be as gradual and responsive as you like, and some families may be ready to consider using these principles at bedtime and nighttime from about four months onwards. If you're stepping away, then it's only for a short period and you'd be actively limiting periods where your baby cries.

For other methods that involve longer periods of letting your baby cry like Cry It Out or the Ferber method (aka Controlled Crying), most families start sleep training around six months. These methods can be effective for some families, but lots of other families struggle emotionally.

This book is about setting sleep foundations in the early days and therefore I don't go through these techniques here. This book is designed to set some great foundations for healthy sleep, and you may therefore not need to select a 'method' to use at six months because sleep is already coming together. For those that like structure and feel happier working towards a 'goal', check out my ladder method below.

On a personal note, sleep training is one area of parenting that totally divides. Social media is full of opinions and can be a very toxic space. Unfollow those accounts if you feel they aren't providing value and aren't aligning with your thoughts and beliefs.

If you choose to sleep train your baby, the method you select will be based on a multitude of factors and influenced by your hormones, driving how you feel and respond when your baby cries. Try not to feel pressure to mimic what other families have done. Try not to change anything that is working for you based on someone else's opinion.

If you want to consider sleep training your baby, read up on different techniques (Or consult me!) and make sure you're confident and happy with the sleep training approach you choose. Even the gentlest of methods can feel hard so it's right you prepare adequately for change.

If you're confident, you'll be consistent. When we introduce changes for our little ones, providing consistency and support is the fairest thing we can do to enable them to learn new skills.

Supporting the development of independent sleep skills: The ladder

Closeness and contact are all your newborn has ever known. They feel absolutely connected to you. You may find they fall asleep easily whilst feeding, being held, in the pram, car seat or whilst baby wearing. This is all very normal and please do not worry about developing 'habits' or 'a rod for your own back' at this stage! In fact, please do embrace the cuddles and the closeness.

The support we give to our child when falling asleep is often more intensive in the early days. Think, feeding, rocking, bouncing, shushing. You can feel a long way off popping them down in their sleep space, saying good night and walking away!

Over the coming months, your baby will grow bigger, stronger, and more able. For those keen to 'work' on setting healthy sleep foundations that lead to independence at night it may help to think about the journey to self-soothing as a ladder with steps to climb.

There is no suggested time to take when progressing through the stages of the ladder. Young babies have a great degree of variability with their sleep so they may need a little more support one day to the next. Gradually, over time, just try to do a little less. See if they can manage to fall asleep in a new way.

Over a period of weeks (or months), you do a little less and your baby does a little more. It is a very natural progression towards independence and self-soothing. You may find you are able to master the top rungs sooner than you think! For many families who work on this gradual technique, they may find they do not need to do any 'formal' sleep training at a later stage.

Try to work on introducing any new elements in the evening. The sleep pressure is greater, plus there's melatonin (for older babies) that can help them to fall asleep easier and embrace new ways of doing things! Once they master the new skills at bedtime, they are easier to repeat during the night (when their other needs have been met) and for naps.

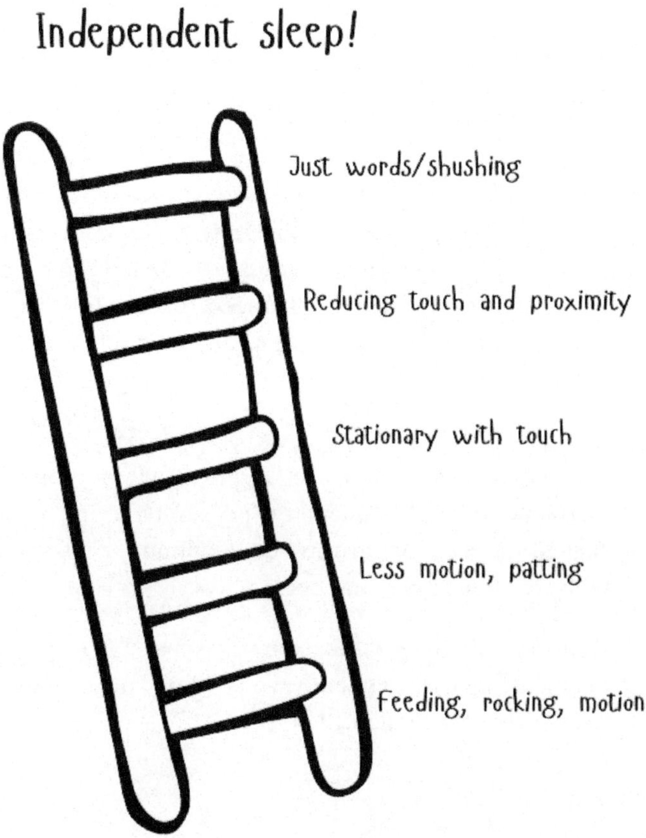

The ladder

1. The first rung of the ladder is helping your baby to fall asleep by feeding or rocking. It is quite intensive.

2. The second rung of the ladder is supporting your baby with less rocking, patting, pacing or a gentle sway. Once you can master these, you do not need to rely so much on rung number one.

3. Climbing the ladder further, we will reduce the motion altogether and enable the baby to fall asleep stationary, either next to you (a side sleeper is great for this) or being held. You may want to continue the patting, as this helps with a smoother transition from being in your arms to being in their cot. You will now not need to rely so much on rung two.

4. Once your baby has stopped relying on motion to soothe, you can work on gradually reducing the touch and/or patting needed to fall asleep. Just a gentle pat or stroke to show it is time to sleep, and then remove your hand. You can continue to use voice and proximity to calm.

5. Once your baby is happy settling by your side, you can gradually work on reducing the proximity, sitting by the side of the cot, or on the bed. Continue to use your voice to show your presence.

6. By now, you are reaching the top rung! Your baby is falling asleep independently, you will be able to reduce the words/shushing needed too.

CHAPTER 3

PERFECT THE SLEEP ENVIRONMENT!

I always start here with my clients when looking at some simple changes and positive steps in the right direction. Consider them easy ticks in the right boxes and then move on.

Darkness. This is so critical to how we function as humans! Darkness serves as a sleepy cue (almost all of you will close the curtains before bed). Darkness also helps the body to produce the hormone melatonin, which helps us sleep. It's certainly worth investing in some good blackout blinds. Darkness also helps minimise distractions and helps keep the room cooler in summer.

White noise. Now, this is also a good sleepy cue, but it helps drown out household noises (Siblings too!) or environmental noises such as the traffic outside. White noise should be loud and consistent for the whole duration of the nap or bedtime rather than played at the initial stages of bedtime or just when falling asleep.

As mentioned earlier, the AAP (American Academy of Pediatrics) (3) recommends white noise volume is set to less than 50dB and that the machine be placed away from your baby's cot. You can download a free decibel meter app on your phone, place it in your baby's cot and measure the volume.

Temperature. Being cold is a common factor for night waking. Being too hot raises the risk of SIDS (sudden infant death syndrome). Investing in a good sleeping bag with clear TOG ratings will help ensure your baby doesn't get too hot or cold. Importantly, sleeping bags also don't come off and travel with even the most restless of sleepers (loose blankets are a SIDS risk). Aim for the room to be 16°C to 20°C (60.8°F to 68°F) and invest in a nursery thermometer.

As a general rule, we want to avoid the polar opposites of icy hands and feet and hot, sweaty babies!

CHAPTER 4
SAFE SLEEP

Sadly, more than 200 babies unexpectedly die of SIDS in the UK each year (4).

SIDS (sudden infant death syndrome – also called crib death or cot death) is extremely rare but absolutely devastating. The good news is that over the years we have seen huge progress in reducing death rates by making minor changes.

SIDS is more common in the first six months of a child's life (88% of cases) and usually occurs when the child is sleeping.

Thankfully, the death rates are falling. Since the Back to Sleep campaign was launched (babies placed on their backs rather than on their fronts in their sleep space) the death rate has fallen by 81%. However, we still don't know what causes it.

For up-to-date advice and guidance on the safest sleep practices in the UK consult The Lullaby Trust (5) or NHS (6) for advice.

16 tips to lower the risk of SIDS

1. Sleeping position: Always place your baby on their back to sleep (until baby rolls easily both back to front and front to back – and even then, continue to put them on their back initially).

2. Baby should sleep on a firm, flat surface (unless otherwise discussed with a medical professional).

3. When your baby falls asleep, place them in the 'feet to foot' position with their feet touching the end of the cot, Moses basket, or pram.

4. Keep the baby's head uncovered.

5. Avoid any loose bedding or too much bedding. Blankets should be tucked in no higher than shoulder level and never near your baby's face. Use a baby sleeping bag if possible.

6. Weighted blankets or weighted sleeping bags are not considered safe (7).

7. Keep the cot clear. Soft toys should be avoided until they're older. Do not use cot bumpers.

8. Think about where your baby sleeps. Let your baby sleep in a cot or Moses basket in the same room as you for the first six months.

9. Do not use a soft mattress. Use a crib mattress that's firm, flat, waterproof and in good condition.

10. Breastfeed your baby if you can.

11. Do not smoke during pregnancy or let anyone smoke in the same room as your baby – both before and after birth.

12. Bedsharing: do not sleep on a bed, sofa or armchair with your baby. If you'd like to co-sleep, there's separate advice on co-sleeping and keeping a safe sleep environment to reduce a baby's risk of SIDS. Check out the Lullaby Trust for this information.

13. Do not sleep in the same bed with your baby if you or your partner smoke or take drugs, or if you've been drinking alcohol.

14. Do not let your baby get too hot or too cold – a room temperature of 16°C to 20°C is ideal with light bedding or a lightweight baby sleeping bag.

15. Don't overwrap your baby and use the right TOG sleep sack for the temperature in your baby's room. Check your baby's neck to ensure they're not getting too hot.

16. Do not use a hot water bottle in bed with your baby.

CHAPTER 5

SLEEPWEAR

This area is dominated by companies trying to sell you the most up-to-date, fashionable, innovative product for your baby to sleep in. Some brands charge high premiums for their products, and honestly, it's just not worth it!

In the early days, swaddling and/or sleeping bags or sleep sacks are the popular methods for helping newborns feel secure and promoting better sleep. Both have their benefits and can be used at various stages of your baby's development. They're preferable to using blankets and sheets as they can't become untucked and cause a SIDS risk.

Remember: Weighted blankets or weighted sleeping bags are not considered safe for sleeping infants (7).

Swaddling

A swaddle is a snug wrap. Your baby's hands will be secured by their sides, or in a more upright position. Swaddling techniques aim to mimic the snugness of the womb, which in turn can calm and soothe newborn babies.

Swaddling also helps to reduce the startle reflex (Moro reflex), which can wake young babies.

How to swaddle safely

If you choose to swaddle you may need some practice first! Make sure to use a lightweight, breathable swaddle.

Practice on a baby doll a few times before trying it on your new baby! When practising, pick a moment when they are calm and relaxed before trying it at sleep time. A guide to the swaddling technique follows.

You can also buy structured swaddles that just involve a zip and/or a Velcro wrap. Honestly, I think these are worth the investment. Some babies manage to wriggle out of their swaddles and the loose blankets can become a risk. Also, zipping up the swaddle after a 3am nappy change is highly preferable to mastering the blanket technique.

TOP TIP! Make sure the swaddle is snug around the arms and chest but loose around the hips and legs to allow for natural hip movement. This helps to prevent hip dysplasia.

How to swaddle a baby: Step-by-step guide

Step 1: Lay out the swaddle

Spread the swaddle on a flat surface in a diamond shape. Fold down the top corner about six inches to form a straight edge.

Step 2: Position your baby

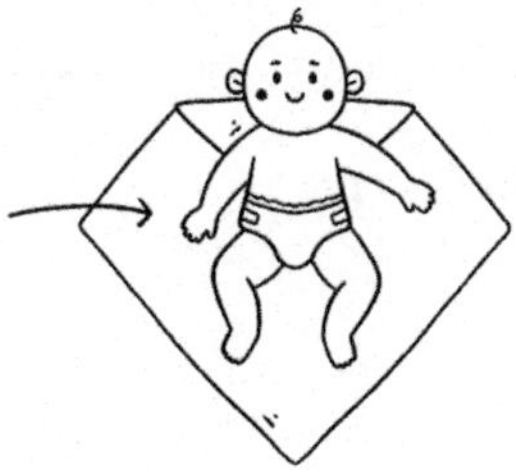

Place your baby on their back with their neck aligned with the folded edge. Make sure your baby's head is above the folded corner and their body is below it.

Step 3: Secure the right arm

Straighten your baby's right arm along their side. Bring the left corner of the swaddle across the baby's body and tuck it under their left side, leaving the left arm free.

Step 4: Fold the bottom

Fold the bottom corner of the swaddle up over the baby's feet and tuck it into the top of the swaddle, ensuring it's snug but not too tight around the hips and legs.

Step 5: Secure the left arm

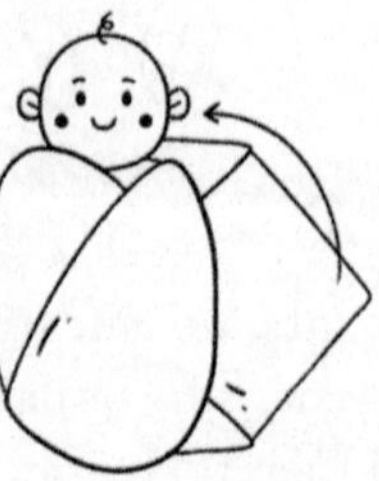

Straighten your baby's left arm and bring the right corner of the swaddle across their body, tucking it under their right side.

Step 6: Final adjustments

Ensure the swaddle is snug around the baby's upper body but loose enough around the hips and legs to allow for natural movement. Make sure the baby's face is uncovered and their neck is not restricted.

When to stop swaddling

Typically, you should stop swaddling by two to three months or when your baby shows signs of rolling over. Then it is time to transition to a sleeping bag. It may feel scary to transition from something that has helped so much.

You have these options:

Cold turkey: Some babies will transition just fine being moved over to a sleeping bag. Other babies may have trouble settling for a couple of nights (and you may need to notch up the soothing techniques) but will then adjust.

One arm first: You can buy transition swaddles where a baby can have one arm out at first. The swaddle will also turn into a sleeping bag. If using a swaddle blanket, you can find one arm techniques online.

Time of day: You may want to try no swaddle at bedtime first, then the rest of the night, then naps.

Sleeping bags

Sleeping bags, sleep sacks, or wearable blankets are sleeveless fabric bags that zip up and secure over the shoulders. They have a TOG rating to guide you by season and provide warmth.

They allow babies to move their arms freely while still offering the security of being enclosed and don't have the same SIDS worries as using loose blankets as they won't cover your baby's face. They are also easy to use and some even have little windows for a quick nappy change!

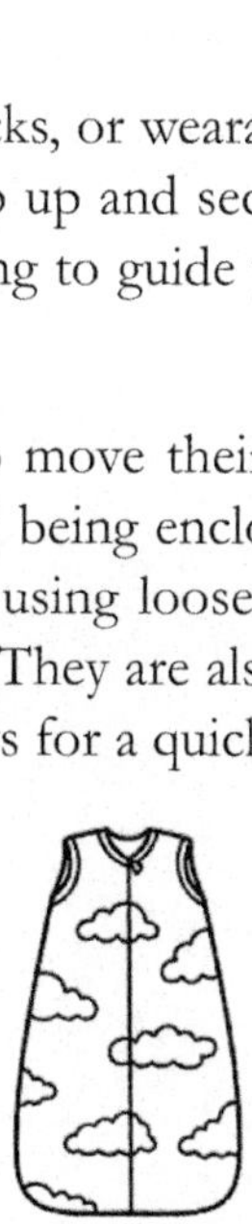

Choosing the right sleep bag

Size: Choose one that fits your baby's size and weight. It should be snug (but not restrictive) around the neck and armholes but spacious enough in the leg area to be hip-healthy.

Material: Choose a fabric and TOG rating appropriate for the season. Organic cotton or muslin can be useful for the warmer temperatures in the summer, and you can get warmer weight sleeping bags with arms for the winter.

Overheating is a SIDS risk. It's tempting to bundle up your little one. Follow the manufacturer's recommendations for your swaddle or sleeping bag.

CHAPTER 6

NIGHT FEEDING

If this is your first baby, going from seven- to nine-hour (often uninterrupted) sleep periods to waking multiple times at night can be a little bit of a shock.

Babies will wake at night for a few reasons:

- Hunger
- Need for comfort and reassurance
- Discomfort (typically a full or dirty nappy)

- Sleep associations (needing support to fall back to sleep).

Night feeds are vital for newborns. They help ensure their nutritional needs are met and blood sugar levels stay regulated.

Newborns have small stomachs. (At birth, they're just the size of a marble!) Therefore, they need small but frequent feedings to get enough calories and nutrients.

For breastfeeding mothers, night feeding helps maintain milk supply and stimulate milk production.

How night feedings change over time

Note: This is highly variable! Your baby's nutritional requirements are unique. There is no right or wrong. Indeed, there will also be periods when your baby feeds more often at night such as when they have growth spurts.

Here is an estimate of night feeds over the coming months.

0–3 Months

Expect to feed your baby every two to three hours around the clock. Newborns typically wake up at night for feedings, as they need to eat about 8–12 times per day. Each feed may take a long time.

3–6 Months

By this stage, some babies might start sleeping for longer stretches at night, but many will still need one to three feedings during the night. Feedings may become shorter as your baby becomes more efficient at feeding.

6 Months+

Some babies can sleep through the night without feeding, while others may still need one or more feedings. If you're considering night weaning, do it gradually. Gradual weaning allows a more natural ending. Reduce the volume or time of each feeding slowly to help your baby adjust.

Night feed tips

Balancing sleep and night feedings can be challenging.

Here are some tips to help you and your baby get more rest:

Hunger or comfort? Try to differentiate between hunger and other causes of waking. If your baby wakes up crying but has recently been fed, they may need soothing and comfort rather than more food.

Dream feeding: Consider offering a dream feed. This is an added feed before you go to bed. This might help your baby sleep a bit longer before waking up for the next feed. The dream feed usually happens around 10pm before you go to bed. You'd pick up your baby whilst still in a sleepy state and offer a feed. Many babies latch well. If your baby sleeps a longer stretch after this feed, then you will too!

A dream feed doesn't work well for every family. Try it for a few days and assess.

Cluster feeding: In the evening, your baby may want to feed more often. This is known as cluster feeding and can help them sleep longer stretches at night.

Look after yourself: Have a drink and snack prepared for you too. It's certainly worth investing in a nursing chair for the room so you're comfortable when feeding your baby at night.

Make sure to pop some slippers and a big robe near to your bed so you get ready first and then don't feel the cold so much. We often tend to our little ones with such urgency, but if we are comfortable then we can provide better care for them!

You may also want to have an eBook reader or audiobook to pass some time, especially if your baby is still slow to feed. If using a phone, make sure to turn it on night mode/night shift to reduce the blue light emitted.

Invest in a small nightlight. Ideally a red colour or one with a 'warmer' light. This will help you see what you're doing and avoid any stubbed toes in the middle of the night.

Tips for breastfeeding at night

Breastfeeding at night offers wonderful opportunities for bonding but can sometimes feel tough for one parent.

Here's some quick tips to make it easier. You may also want to visit your local breastfeeding support group or La Leche League who will be able to provide more comprehensive advice and support if you're struggling with day or night feeds.

Side sleepers: Having your baby sleep in a bassinet or crib in your room can make night feedings more convenient. You can get side sleepers that give your baby a separate sleep space attached to your bed. This will make transferring them from their sleep space to breast (and back again) much easier.

Positioning: A side-lying position can be comfortable for nighttime breastfeeding. It allows you to rest while your baby nurses.

Nighttime milk: If your baby sleeps for longer stretches and you need to support your milk supply, consider pumping at night. This can help you store milk for future use if you choose to add in bottle feeds. Nighttime breastmilk also contains Melatonin (the sleepy hormone) so label it as special sleepy night milk!

Tips for bottle-feeding at night

Efficient bottle-feeding at night requires a little prep!

Preparation: Prepare bottles in advance by measuring the formula, using ready-made formula or a prep machine. You may want to set up a little bottle prep zone in the bedroom to save the walk to the kitchen.

Share the load: If possible, share night feeding duties with your partner. Taking turns can help both of you get more rest. You may find it more restful to do one night on one night off rather than alternate feeds.

CHAPTER 7
BABY SLEEP POSITIONS

What are the best positions for baby sleep?

As we discussed in the last chapter, sleeping safely with your baby is a top priority for parents and is central to all the advice I give.

Here's a little reminder of the basics for baby sleeping positions. The NHS (6) and the Lullaby Trust (4) state the safest place for a baby to sleep is on their back, on a separate firm sleep surface, such as a cot or Moses basket. No soft bedding, pillows, or toys.

Why? Well, since the Back to Sleep campaign started, this position has been shown to significantly reduce the risk of sudden infant death syndrome (SIDS) (7).

Safe baby sleeping positions: A recap

Ensuring your baby sleeps safely is paramount. The following guidelines are essential for creating a safe sleep environment:

1. Always place your baby on their back to sleep for naps and nighttime. This position is the safest and reduces the risk of SIDS.

2. Use a firm mattress covered with a fitted sheet. Avoid soft surfaces like couches, armchairs, or adult beds.

3. Keep the cot free of soft objects, toys, pillows, and loose bedding. These items pose a suffocation risk.

4. Room share: Share your room with your baby for at least the first six months to reduce the risk of SIDS. Side sleepers are great for keeping your baby in their own sleep space but close enough for easy night feeds.

5. Dress your baby in light sleep clothing and keep the room at a comfortable temperature. Overheating can increase the risk of SIDS.

Early rolling? The newborn scrunch or newborn curl

Many parents quite rightly panic if they notice their newborn rolling to their side during sleep. This position, often referred to as the 'newborn scrunch' or 'newborn curl' might look like the baby is starting to learn to roll.

However, this is typically a natural reflex rather than an intentional movement. Newborns tend to curl up into a fetal position, which can cause them to roll to their side.

Despite this reflex, it's important to always place your baby on their back to sleep. If you notice your baby has rolled to their side, gently roll them back. Consistently placing your baby on their back helps establish safe sleep habits and reduces the risk of SIDS.

When babies learn to roll: 'Getting stuck'

This is a big milestone to reach! As babies grow and develop their motor skills, they begin to experiment with rolling. During this phase, it is very common for babies to roll to their side at nighttime and get 'stuck'. Getting stuck in one position can be frustrating for the baby and can lead to them crying out for support and an increase in night waking.

Apart from giving you some gentle reassurance that this phase will pass when they finally master the skill, here's what you can do to help:

1. Continue to offer supervised tummy time in the day. This helps develop the muscles that are essential for rolling both ways.

2. Keep an eye on your baby when they are trying to roll. If they get stuck on their side, try to help them complete the roll. Use the opportunity to teach the skill. If they're really stuck, then assist them by rolling them back.

3. Don't be tempted by sleep positioners or wedges to keep your baby in a specific position. They are not safe for sleep.

When is it safe for a baby to sleep on their front or side?

It is generally not safe for babies to sleep on their front or side until they have reached certain developmental milestones. As we know, all babies develop at different rates so here's what you need to consider:

1. Continue placing your baby on their back to sleep for all naps and nighttime sleep until they are at least one year old. This position is the safest and significantly reduces the risk of SIDS.

2. Once your baby can roll over from back to front and front to back confidently on their own, it is usually safe for them to sleep in the position they choose. At this stage, they have developed the necessary motor skills to adjust their position during sleep, which helps prevent suffocation. However, still place them on their back when you put them down.

3. Even when your baby starts rolling both ways confidently, continue to ensure their sleep environment is safe. Use a firm mattress, avoid soft bedding, and keep the cot free of toys and pillows.

My baby has reflux, what's the best sleeping position?

Babies with reflux often experience discomfort when lying flat on their back. The management of reflux can be complicated and should be discussed with your child's health professional before making any adjustments to their sleeping position.

They may suggest:

1. A slight incline: elevating the head of the cot slightly. The incline is gentle, and the baby remains on their back. However, the evidence behind this is poor and advice mixed. The Lullaby Trust, the NHS and the American Academy of Pediatrics do not recommend it. Remember a firm, flat surface is the general recommendation, so this should only be changed with medical advice.

2. A period of being held upright before being placed back down. Holding your baby upright for 20–30 minutes after feeding may help reduce reflux symptoms and make it more comfortable when placed on their back for sleep after a feed.

My baby has wind/gas pains, what's the best sleeping position?

This is common during the newborn stages and for babies starting to wean. A build-up of wind/gas can cause discomfort and disrupt a baby's sleep. Here are some positions to help alleviate wind:

1. Continue with a back sleeping position. While on their back, gently moving their legs in a bicycling motion can help release wind.

2. While babies should not sleep on their stomachs, supervised tummy time while they are awake can help relieve wind before nap or bedtime. This position helps strengthen their muscles and can move those bubbles of wind through the body.

3. Brief periods of side lying while the baby is awake and supervised can also help relieve wind. Always ensure they return to their back for sleep.

Ensuring a safe sleeping environment for your baby is paramount. Their sleeping position is important.

Always prioritise placing your baby on their back to sleep, use a firm sleep surface, and avoid soft bedding. Special considerations for reflux and wind can be managed with slight adjustments, but always under the guidance of a health professional who will be able to offer personalised advice for your baby.

Safe sleep practices not only protect your baby but also provide peace of mind for parents.

CHAPTER 8
DUMMY/ PACIFIER USE

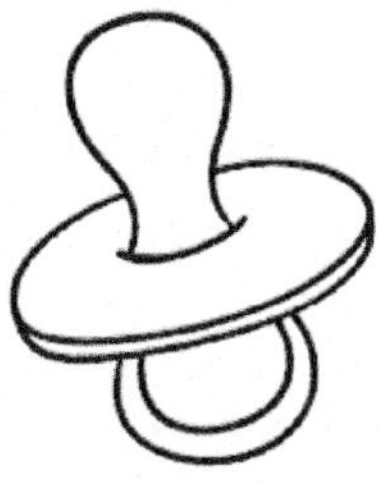

There's no doubt about it, babies are born with a powerful desire to suck to soothe. Some babies will get instantaneous relief from a dummy whereas other babies find comfort in other things and just seem disinterested, often spitting it back out.

For babies who love their dummy, it brings them comfort, and it's likely with that comfort they can soothe, calm, and drift off to sleep. Fabulous!

However, as they enter the deeper stages of sleep, their muscles relax, and the dummy is likely to fall out.

Okay, so, what does this mean in reality?

Typically, one of two things will happen:

- They'll stay asleep (amazing).
- They will wake up (not so amazing).

If they wake, it may be either immediately or after their first sleep cycle. If the baby doesn't notice, great! It's likely to be a helpful sleep aid. However, if they wake either immediately or soon after it falls out then we need to rethink how 'helpful' it is.

Dummy issues

Some babies can only resettle when the dummy is put back in, and with this, they form a sleep association and need it to drift back off to sleep. I speak to many parents who find themselves 're-plugging' all night long and it can be tiring.

Now, I was a 're-plugger' myself. I chose to do this with my little girl. Her reflux was so terrible, and the dummy brought her such relief that I was 'plugging it' back in until she was old enough to do this for herself. This skill can usually be mastered between seven to nine months of age. It's what works for you as a family, weighing up the pros and cons.

Is the dummy harmful?

No! It brings a huge amount of comfort to many children. Whilst there have been concerns raised about excessive dummy use causing dental issues and interference with speech development, if we limit dummy use to just naps and nighttime, that helps. There have also been concerns (9) about a dummy causing ear infections, so maintaining proper dummy hygiene (including sterilisation for a young baby) is important.

So, to avoid any unwanted complications, ideally, you would be using a dummy to settle for naps and at nighttime and removing it in the morning.

Want to get rid of their dummy?

If you choose to ditch the dummy, there are options from cold turkey to taking a more gradual approach. As with all children growing up, the way we go about things depends on their age and level of understanding.

For a baby under six months

If they're less than six months old, it's often better to go cold turkey when ditching the dummy.

Yes, they may need a little extra help falling asleep for naps and your nights may be a little disrupted for a few days but then it's gone. Stick with it, be consistent and help them find other ways to seek comfort. For example, you could have your hand on their tummy as they fall asleep or pick them up to soothe them before placing them back down.

At this age, little ones don't have long-term memory and haven't formed an emotional attachment to their dummy in the same way older children do. You may find they seek comfort in other ways such as sucking on a thumb or their wrist.

If they're young and still swaddled, then swaddle with one arm out so they've got easy reach to their hands to help them soothe.

Over six months?

So, what are some tips if they're six months and up? Babies have often started to develop more of an emotional attachment and will 'miss it' more. You can still get rid of it at this age, but the protests are likely to be for longer and could be a little louder!

You can still go cold turkey or reduce to one nap/sleep a day and then gradually wean from that when you feel they are ready for the transition.

CHAPTER 9

How Much Sleep Do Babies Need?

Note: The first thing to mention about infant sleep is that it's highly variable and this is completely normal in terms of normal sleep development!

Whilst I've tried to illustrate a typical picture, your baby may fall asleep outside these windows and may need more or less sleep than quoted.

Babies' sleep needs are completely individual and are affected by their development, environment and growth. Just like every other aspect of caring for our babies, we learn their needs alongside them.

Newborns (0–3 months old)

Overview: Please don't worry about introducing a set 'by the clock' routine at this stage for your newborn baby. Their body clock and circadian rhythm just aren't established yet. Ten-minute naps will be common as well as naps lasting hours at a time! Sleep patterns can be very irregular.

Most newborn babies will continue to wake multiple times at night for feeds and comfort and the boundary between day and night isn't clear. It's common for babies to have night and day confusion and no set pattern at all. As a result, bedtime may be very late, or even feel like it doesn't quite happen at all!

What to expect: 16–17 hours total sleep in 24 hours, multiple naps, 30- to 90-minute wake windows, multiple night feeds.

How much sleep does my three-month-old need?

Overview: Many babies will have started to 'wake to the world' now that they're out of those early weeks. However, sleep still remains highly variable at this age. Typically, they will take around five naps in the day.

At around 8–12 weeks we welcome the production of their own melatonin! Melatonin has a soporific effect and will help with feeling sleepy at bedtime. You may start to see some more consistency and longer stretches of sleep at night. You may want to start experimenting with the simple steps of a bedtime routine to introduce some good healthy sleep habits and sleep cues.

What to expect: 16–17 hours total sleep in 24 hours, multiple naps, 30- to 90-minute wake windows, multiple night feeds.

Sleep requirements at four to five months old

Overview: The four-month regression hits (although this can actually be anywhere between three to five months). More 'adult-like' sleep cycles start to develop. Typically, this is characterised by a change in sleep patterns and trouble sleeping.

Sleep now moves through a more distinct sleep cycle with several stages called REM and NREM sleep. This can introduce new sleep problems with disturbed nights and possibly frequent re-settles. Not all babies will be as affected by the regression and some babies will start sleeping longer stretches.

What to expect: 14–16 hours a day, 3–4 naps, 1.5- to 2.5-hour wake windows, night feeds, more distinct daytime 'pattern'.

How much sleep does my five- to seven-month-old need?

Overview: Typically, we'll start to see the transition from four to three naps a day. Some babies will be sleeping longer stretches at night with one or two feeds (depending on development).

Other babies will start sleeping through the night. The daytime schedule becomes far more predictable, and naps may start to become more reliable. At least one nap of the day may lengthen (consolidate).

Your baby may need less help to fall asleep and stay asleep and may be able to settle and get back to sleep if they wake at night and don't need feeding or changing.

What to expect: 14–15 hours a day, 3–4 naps, 2- to 3-hour wake windows, fewer night feeds, distinct daytime 'pattern'.

What happens to sleep at seven to nine months of age?

Overview: Commonly, we'll see changes to sleep at night (aka the eight-month regression). Usually, babies are going through a big developmental growth period, learning to crawl or pull up.

Separation anxiety can also creep in, and this can affect night sleep. Plus, there's a nap transition and there are also teeth! Argh. Teeth. There are always teeth!

You'll also probably find the last nap of the day is dropped and they'll transition to a clearer two-nap schedule with a morning and early afternoon nap. They may need an earlier bedtime temporarily when making this transition.

Babies may be able to go through the night without a night feed (still highly variable and dependent on many factors).

What to expect: 14–15 hours in 24 hours, 2–3 naps, 2.5- to 3.5-hour wake windows, less night feeds, distinct daytime 'pattern'.

At 9–15 months, transition to toddlerhood

Overview: Hurrah! We have a brief window of stability on a two-nap day schedule. Sometimes children may look ready to drop their first nap around 12 months of age, but it's more likely to be a bit of a separation anxiety phase and some acute FOMO! Quite frankly, they'd much rather be playing than napping.

Most children are better set to dropping the first nap of the day from 14 months onwards.

Most children will be able to sleep for much longer stretches at night and sleeping through the night (or long periods) is an achievable goal for many parents to aim for.

This is a huge period of growth and development, and you may notice them practising their skills in the middle of the night!

What to expect: 14–15 hours a day, 3–4 naps, 2- to 3-hour wake windows, fewer/no night feeds, distinct day-time 'pattern'.

Older toddlers: 15–18 months to 2.5 years

Overview: Another period of change when your little toddler is highly likely to transition to one long nap in the middle of their day. With any change, there may be a period of instability. Bring bedtime earlier if they're struggling with the longer wake windows.

What to expect: 12–14 hours in 24 hours, 1 nap, 5- to 6-hour wake windows.

Sleep requirements for three- to five-year-olds (the pre-school years)

Overview: Most toddlers will be able to drop their lunch-time nap around the age of 2.5–3.5. Some will need a nap for a little longer and some will be ready to drop it sooner.

For older children, replace the nap with some quiet time to allow them the opportunity to rest and recover. An early bedtime will help make this transition a little easier and avoid overtiredness during the bedtime routine.

What to expect: 10.5–13 hours in 24 hours, 0–1 nap, 6- to 12-hour wake windows.

CHAPTER 10
NAPS

Naptime brings relief, allowing your baby to rest and for you to have a bit of downtime, or just catch up on the million other things on the to-do list. Daily naps provide your little one with some much-needed rest throughout the day. Think about your child's growth, it is so exhausting.

Naps allow those little bodies to recover and brains to process everything they've learnt. In addition to supporting growth and development, they're helpful for a whole range of other things:

- Cognitive function, memory consolidation
- Boosts your immune system
- Can improve motor skill development
- Reduce stress and anxiety and improve mood (lower cortisol levels)
- Improved attention and focus.

Naps are as important as sleep at night and give us our total sleep duration (day sleep + sleep at night).

Newborn babies' naptime schedules can be completely erratic or nocturnal, possibly spending more time sleeping during the day than at night in the early stages.

Gradually, over the next 12–18 months, you'll watch as they grow older and stronger. They will be able to manage longer periods of awake time between naps and get through to bedtime without becoming tired and fussy.

Then they will transition to one good sleep period in the middle of the day, and most tend to grow out of naptime completely around the three-year-old mark.

How long should naps be?

In the early weeks, naps can be anywhere from ten minutes to two hours or more. This makes aiming for a daily schedule pretty impossible.

When babies have passed the four-month regression and their sleep is in more distinctive 'sleep cycles' you'll start to notice a 45-minute (or so) pattern forming with a baby waking after that period. They may wake refreshed or upset and need a little help getting back to sleep.

Shorter naps (cat naps) can be problematic for babies who constantly wake up upset after a short period of time and struggle to make it through to the next nap.

Naps should consolidate (when sleep cycles stitch together) and lengthen over time. This isn't easy for most babies and takes a bit of practice. It's more achievable by six months of age.

Most families like to cap naps around the two-hour mark to stop any longer daytime naps affecting nighttime sleep.

Naptime routine

Now, this doesn't have to be complicated. However, a short naptime routine will go far! Try to include some familiar elements from your bedtime routine so your baby benefits from similar sleep cues and will start understanding what's coming next.

If you can, consider their sleep environment. It's worth trying to step away from the hustle and bustle of the day with all the distractions going on. We all find it hard to unwind after a busy day, and the same applies to babies. Try to factor in a 10- to 15-minute wind-down before a nap at home.

Three top tips to get baby to nap

1. **Think of the ideal sleep environment.** You'll probably want to invest in some good blackout curtains or blinds. Sunlight can make the sleep environment bright; your little one may be distracted by their surroundings. (In Summer, blackout curtains also help keep the room cool.)

2. **Be realistic and have a good plan B!** If you're working on extending naps or your baby's nap schedule and getting enough sleep, then it may be worth knowing when to reach out for the plan B.

It's great to work on independent sleep, but if you've been working on a single nap unsuccessfully for a while then it may be best to take a break for 10–15 minutes, and then try again.

Or you can offer a little more support. That may be assisting your baby to sleep (feeding, rocking, patting) or using motion (lots of babies will sleep well in a pram or car seat).

For little babies, if naptimes and sleep patterns have been all over the place then just getting your little one through to bedtime (without becoming too fussy) will be the priority.

3. **Watch wake windows.** Especially for little ones. Working on a baby nap schedule is HARD. However, some of the pressure is taken off when we start to look at wake windows. When the window is drawing to a close, aim for a little wind-down to get them to sleep. This helps avoid both under-tired and over-tired scenarios. You can see the suggested wake windows in the previous chapter.

CHAPTER 11

Surviving the Four-Month Sleep Regression

Has your baby stopped sleeping soundly? Are they not falling asleep like they used to or taking short naps? Is the bedtime routine now a struggle, or have they started waking frequently at night…?

Hello, four-month sleep regression!

The four-month sleep regression may actually happen anywhere around the three- to five-month mark. If your baby is premature, sleep is calculated from their adjusted age. This may be completely different to how they previously slept a couple of weeks ago, or it may have always been bad and it's just got worse!

Not all babies will 'hit' the four-month sleep regression. All babies will pass this milestone, but like everything, some will sail through, and others will feel it a little more.

Technically, this isn't much of a regression at all. It's a huge physical leap in your baby's sleep and a big developmental milestone.

Is this sleep regression normal? Sleep, cycles and stages

Sleep has various 'stages'.

In the newborn stage, babies fall asleep and stay asleep in a pretty much constant fashion, with no real cycles, just some active sleep (where you notice their little eyelids moving around) and some quiet sleep. They then tend to wake for milk, because they're uncomfortable (nappy change) or they've simply had enough sleep.

Newborns also don't produce much melatonin of their own, making their circadian rhythm (body clock) rather unpredictable. You may notice that day-night sleep is confused, and they sleep longer stretches for naps than their night sleep.

As adults, we progress through distinct stages or sleep cycles throughout the night. The stages are REM and non-REM sleep. Non-REM sleep is then also made up of different stages.

Essentially, we go from an awake state to drowsy to light sleep, then deep sleep, and then back into the lighter sleep stages. We then have a *partial waking* before transitioning into the next sleep cycle.

REM sleep is the 'dreaming stage', it helps support learning and development, and the brain processes the events from the day.

Non-REM sleep is more restful and restorative. The body can repair. The deeper sleep states help you wake feeling refreshed. If you're woken in the deepest sleep state, you can feel disorientated.

The partial waking serves as a bit of a protective mechanism. We wake, check everything out, and if it's okay then we fall back to sleep. If we notice a change or a problem, then we will wake up fully. As adults, we'd probably notice if our partner had disappeared, or if the landing light was on, whereas when we went to bed it was off. Small changes in our environment can trigger full wakes.

For a baby or child, they're likely to wake fully (rather than progress into another sleep cycle) if they find themselves in a different place, eg they fell asleep in your arms and now they are in their cot. Or if they were feeding and now they're not.

Around the four-month mark, babies transition between two sleep phases (active and quiet) to cycling between REM and non-REM sleep with partial wakings.

Why does the four-month sleep regression happen?

Perhaps your zero- to three-month-old was having some wonderfully long stretches of sleep. Then your beautiful sleeping baby changes… but this period is completely normal.

The change may look different for each family but typically their sleep patterns will change. They may have difficulty falling asleep for naps or nights, wake often (sometimes every 30 minutes), and seem to have 'lost' their ability to self-soothe.

If your little one is now giving you sleepless nights, they might be going through the four-month regression.

Here are some telltale signs to look out for:

- Your baby is waking up more frequently than usual without any obvious reason.
- They're busy practising new skills during the day, like rolling over.
- They suddenly seem much more aware and attentive to their surroundings.
- Maybe they're getting easily distracted while eating or finding it hard to nod off anywhere other than their crib.
- They're taking shorter cat naps.

At this point in your baby's life, they start having more 'adult-like' sleep cycles, lasting around 45 minutes to an hour. As discussed in the previous section, the adult sleep cycle consists of stages of sleep called non-REM and REM sleep.

At the end of each sleep cycle, your baby will have a partial waking. We do this as well. If there's no change to your sleep environment, you'll close your eyes and fall asleep again.

However, if you currently have sleep associations that help you fall asleep, whether that's rocking, feeding, motion, patting etc then you'll wake fully and look for that sleep association to be 'restored' before being able to fall back to sleep.

The same is true for all children four months or older. I work with many families who have toddlers and preschoolers. If a parent remains in the room as their child falls asleep, the child wakes later on and goes huh?! Where are they?! They'll then cry, or if old enough, get out of bed to find you. This, combined with bouts of separation anxiety, can cause sleep problems and disturbed nights.

If your baby starts to learn more independent sleep skills, then they'll wake in the same environment that they fell asleep in and won't look for another feed or to be rocked or held. They're more likely to fall back to sleep independently and transition through the partial waking.

One of the tricky elements of the four-month sleep regression is that many parents don't quite know what it is when it hits them! So, we may put the increased feedings down to a growth spurt or teething. After a few nights of feeding our baby back to sleep, they get rather used to it. Then your baby's sleep habits start to change, and their sleep-wake cycle can involve feeding back to sleep multiple times at night.

For families that recognise the change in their baby's sleep patterns, this regression may last a few days or even two to six weeks.

Seven healthy sleep habits to survive the four-month sleep regression

Try incorporating these seven healthy sleep habits into your routine. These tips not only promote better sleep for your little one, but they also create a peaceful and soothing environment for both you and your baby.

1. Establish a consistent bedtime routine. Creating a consistent bedtime routine for your little one not only helps establish a sense of structure but also leads to better sleep. By providing clear and calming cues, such as a warm bath and a soothing lullaby, your baby can learn to associate these activities with winding down for the day.

   Plus, having their own sleep space can promote a sense of independence and comfort, leading to a peaceful night's rest for all.

2. Are they really hungry? If you're feeding them every 30 minutes, or they're only taking small sips and falling back asleep, then it's more likely to be a sleep association. What's their feeding pattern in the day?

   Even if your baby feeds frequently, perhaps you could expect them to do at least two hours at night without needing a feed. Therefore, any wakes within a couple of hours could be more confidently resettled without a feed.

3. Introduce your little one to new experiences. On well-rested days when you have a bit more energy, it's the perfect time to introduce your little one to new experiences and skills.

   Building good sleep habits may require some experimentation and tinkering, but it's all worth it in the end. I hear parents say they just popped to the loo and came back and their baby was asleep! Whilst that's a pipe dream for some, keep seeking out those opportunities for growth, development and practice, both for the baby's sake and your sanity.

4. Build familiarity with their sleep space. The more your baby sleeps and naps in their sleep space the better. Even if your daily routine involves a lot of running around, making time for a mid-morning or mid-afternoon nap in their cot can make all the difference.

   Familiarity brings comfort. The more familiar it feels, the less the baby will need your help when they wake.

5. Nail that sleep environment. Transforming your baby's sleep routine can be challenging, especially if they struggle with partial wakings. However, by creating a unique and calming sleep environment, you can help reduce these disturbances.

   Setting up a room with minimal light, adding soothing white noise, and maintaining a consistent temperature between 16°C and 20°C can all contribute to better sleep.

6. Avoid overtiredness. Being a new parent is not an easy job, especially when it comes to managing your baby's sleep schedule. Over-tiredness can be a real nightmare, making it almost impossible for your baby to drift off and stay asleep. They may be just too fussy. Offer an extra nap or an earlier bedtime if needed.

7. Manage your expectations. For sure, we all know someone whose baby slept through the night from the moment they were born. However, sleep is not linear, and sleep regressions typically affect most babies at some point.

> Babies start sleeping 'more predictably' from five to six months old after the four-month sleep regression has settled and they've moved on in their sleep development. However, waking at night remains completely normal in this age group.

Most parents experience sleep deprivation of sorts as they support their baby to sleep in the first months or years of life.

Whilst it's great to hold or feed your baby to sleep, at some point, you may want to try and teach them some more independent sleep skills with some gentle sleep training.

When they're falling asleep independently on a more consistent basis, you'll start to see longer stretches emerge at night too.

CHAPTER 12

Illness and Sleep

As a parent, it's heart-breaking to see your little one feeling unwell. It's so hard to comfort them while meeting all their other needs and also trying to help them get the rest they need. Sometimes it can be overwhelming.

It's no surprise that when a baby is sick it can disrupt sleep. Those little bodies are working overtime to fight off the infection and illness, which can lead to more frequent waking in the night for care needs to be met. They're also likely to have a high temperature or fever, which is really miserable! Not forgetting the addition of general discomfort with nausea or rashes such as chicken pox.

Addressing the underlying issue is a key step towards achieving consistent night sleep outcomes in the future. Make sure you've discussed their condition with their GP or other suitable professional, but reassuringly, most general childhood conditions can be managed in the comfort of your home.

Offering extra comfort to your sick baby can not only make them feel better generally, but a happier baby will sleep and feed better too. Remember, stress and anxiety can make it difficult for a baby to fall asleep when they are ill so try to remain positive and happy when around your baby (I know this is hard when they're sick!), emotions can transfer.

Common illnesses affecting baby sleep

Colds, ear infections, and fevers are common childhood illnesses that can affect your baby's sleep.

These common illnesses can cause discomfort and disrupt sleep, making it challenging for your little one to get the rest they need. Babies are especially prone to more frequent illnesses as their immune systems are underdeveloped.

Not to mention the plethora of colds and infections when they start mixing with others in daycare settings! If you're unsure (ie if it's not just the common cold) then calling 111, or visiting your pharmacist or GP will help identify the specific illness your baby is experiencing.

Once you know this, you will be able to provide the right kind of comfort and care they need to recover and sleep better.

How illness affects baby sleep quality

Illness can have two polar effects. It can lead to an increase in your baby's sleep needs, or conversely a difficulty in maintaining sleep, thus affecting their sleep quality and hindering their recovery.

If your baby's nap extends beyond the duration of their usual nap, it is appropriate to check on them first, you'll probably be able to check their nappy and take their temperature whilst still sleeping.

If you're worried, wake them and seek medical attention if necessary. Otherwise, let them catch up on their rest. You may choose to sit nearby whilst they rest.

Making sure your baby is well-fed and hydrated underpins healthy sleep when sick. Breast milk or formula can be a source of comfort and nutrition during this time.

Your GP or Pharmacist may also advise using rehydration salts such as Dioralyte if they've also been suffering from vomiting and/or diarrhoea.

It's worth saying to trust your parenting gut instinct on this one too! Sometimes we 'just know' or have a 'niggling feeling' it's not right. Trust your instincts, you'll be picking up on some small cues and can act on them quickly.

Creating a comfortable sleep environment for a sick baby

Creating a comfortable sleep environment for your sick baby involves maintaining optimal temperature and humidity levels, as well as providing soothing sounds and darkness.

Monitoring the temperature and humidity levels in your baby's room is helpful, especially if they are congested. Some baby monitors will be able to do all this for you!

You may also want to be closer to your baby or child when they're unwell. If they're under six months, likely, they'll still be sharing a room with you, and you can respond quickly if they're unwell at night.

Camping Out: If they're older and in their own room, you may want to consider setting up a camp bed in their room for night sleep. This will help keep them in their familiar sleep environment, but you will be able to provide comfort and reassurance more quickly. It also means they don't need to change their own bed for another, and that familiarity will help provide comfort.

During illness, flexibility with baby's sleep schedules and prioritising rest and recovery for your baby is crucial. Your baby may require more restful days with shorter wake windows and longer naps, or they may need the same amount of activity as usual as a distraction from feeling rubbish is always helpful!

Providing comfort measures like suctioning of the nose, using a humidifier, and administering Calpol or Ibuprofen (always following recommended dosages) may help promote rest for a poorly infant.

Following your baby's cues and adjusting their sleep schedule accordingly supports their healing process and ensures they get the rest they need.

CHAPTER 13
TRANSITIONING TO THEIR OWN ROOM

A guide for consideration at six months.

Just a reminder that the NHS and other organisations such as the AAP (American Academy of Pediatrics) recommend room sharing until your baby is at least six months of age. This helps to reduce the risk of SIDS by up to 50%.

Many parents choose to transition their baby to their new room around six months of age when the SIDS risk reduces slightly. Most parents will move their child at some point before their first birthday. Some families choose to room share for longer, and in the end, it's a unique decision for each family.

This is a personal decision, try not to be influenced by what 'others' have done. Try to be comfortable and feel confident with your decision when moving your baby to their new bedroom.

Our son, Charlie, had a range of health issues from birth, meaning that moving him to his room at six months wasn't possible. We simply wouldn't have been able to keep him safe. We moved him closer to a year when his health improved. Equally, I needed to be in a better place mentally to trust he would sleep safely and consequently allow my own body to relax into sleep!

Do babies sleep better in their own room?

Well, yes and no. Honestly, it depends on how your baby slept before you made the transition and even thought about moving your baby!

The first six months can be a bit of a roller coaster in terms of baby sleep. Days and nights may be mixed up, managing multiple night feeds, issues with gas/wind, teeth, and learning to roll. (Not to mention the four-month regression!) Needless to say, after the baby arrives, sleep will look very different for quite a while.

Some babies fall into great sleep habits and routines pretty easily, while others take time and require more support from their caregivers. If your baby sleeps well before the move, then they'll probably continue to sleep well in a separate room. There may be a little transition period in between, but the shift will be easier than a baby who is waking multiple times and won't sleep for long stretches.

Equally, what's the current set-up? Are they in their own sleep space or are you bed-sharing? You may find it's easier to first transition from bed-sharing to a separate sleep space and then transition to a separate room.

There is research (10) that reports we sleep better (measured by longer stretches) in separate rooms. However, as with most sleep-related research, there are points open for debate!

In short, if we are in the same room, we may be more likely to wake each other. They obviously wake you, but you can also wake them! Your baby may wake when they hear a parent coming to bed at night. Or, as adults, we may respond (too) quickly. When in fact, had the baby been given a few more moments they may have fallen back to sleep by themselves.

Some babies are particularly restless sleepers. Shimmying, shuffling, squeaking etc. That may keep the parents awake, but equally some adults are like this too and it may be the reverse.

How can I help my baby transition to their new room?

Spend time in their room playing during the day first. It can help them recognise the environment and it can start to feel more familiar.

Perhaps perform nappy changes and other tasks in their room. If you have a chair in the room then take a seat for a bit, read some stories, or feed them.

You can continue to build up time in their room, and do one or more of these suggestions:

- Start performing the bedtime routine in their new room. Then settle them for sleep in the same room as yourself.
- You can move their new cot from the nursery into the shared room so they become more familiar with that in your room first.
- Daytime naps: Try one nap a day in their new room. You could try the first nap of the day. You may need to support your baby to fall asleep if they notice their new environment. If they do well, then increase the number of naps in their new space.
- Try continuing from the bedtime routine and settle them for the first part of their night's sleep in their nursery. You can transfer them to the parent's room when you go to bed at night or after their first waking.

If you'd like to continue room sharing and/or co-sleeping

Awesome! There is NO pressure to move your child to their room. In fact, in many parts of the world, bed or room sharing with babies is expected.

For many families, room sharing suits them better as they can continue to meet their child's needs at night (such as feeding) without going too far.

As I mentioned earlier, if your child has additional needs, as my son did, and a transition would put them at risk then don't consider this an option right now. You can move your baby to their room at any point when it feels right for your family.

If your child isn't ready to night-wean or you wish to continue breastfeeding at night for comfort, then you may wish to consider room sharing for a few months more to make the night feeding feel a little easier.

However, some families will also have a set up in their baby's room, such as a single bed near their cot as a halfway transition.

What you need to consider when moving your baby into their own room

When you've decided your baby has outgrown their current sleep space, you may start thinking it's time to move your baby.

If you feel ready, here are some points to consider:

- Think about creating a comfortable temperature in the room. A temperature between 16°C to 20°C is best. You may want to check the temperature in the room during the night too. Many monitors now have thermometers on them.
- Master the pre-sleep routine in their new room rather than your own. This will help make the transition to the cot more seamless, but also, they won't be 'leaving' their sleep environment for a new one which may feel unfamiliar.
- Try letting your baby nap in their new bed for a few days first, just to build up familiarity with the cot.
- Think about the placement of the baby monitor in the room so you can check on them at night and see if they need your assistance.

- Wondering whether to leave bedroom doors open? This is very much a personal decision. If the hallway will let a lot of light into the room, then you may consider closing the door to keep a nice dark sleep space, or you may want to leave the doors ajar to feel more connected and hear your baby more easily. It's up to you.

CHAPTER 14

TRAVEL AND SLEEP

I know you want to do your best to help your baby sleep, but first of all, I want to say to you: Don't worry too much. You are on holiday. It's such a short time when your number one priority should be FUN.

If you throw out all your routines and sleep schedules during your travels and develop other methods to get your kids to sleep, that's okay – and anything but a problem.

Flying with children

If you are planning a long-haul trip, I would suggest planning a night flight if possible. Your baby will get the longest sleep, and you will have the most relaxed time.

Pack their comforters, sleeping bags and anything else that offers familiarity. The familiar smells of their sleeping bag and comforter can bring comfort. Sure, sleep won't be perfect and may even be later than normal, but it will come eventually and eat up some of the many hours of flying. The gentle movement of the plane and the natural white noise can help your child sleep.

For small children, check the possibility of a bassinet or having a reclining seat on board and book it well in advance with the airline.

If you arrive tired at your destination, take a nap together on the day of arrival and go to bed early. If this isn't a possibility (say, it's already late afternoon), head towards natural light and fresh air, and have a small snack. It'll help the whole family stay awake until you can take an early bedtime at a more appropriate time for your nighttime sleep to start.

Tip #1 At your hotel room, create a place like home:

Whether you are staying with friends, in self-catering accommodation or a hotel, there are always a few things you can do to make their sleep space as comfortable as home.

The best way to do this is to use white noise on a mobile phone or iPad, take their comforter, stuffed animal, sleeping bag/sleep sack and even your child's mattress cover. It should have been used for a few days so it smells like your own bed.

You may be able to use a hotel room crib if booked in advance, and the change may be exciting for your child, but the same bedding should provide familiarity and comfort.

Tip #2 Take advantage of the time zones:

Depending on your time difference, find out which routine works best for you.

Last year, as a family we visited Greece. There it was two hours earlier than in London. We managed to keep the kids on British time the whole holiday. This allowed us to sleep in and have some cozy longer evenings with entertainment at the hotel.

If you can, keep your kids in their original time zone or only adjust them halfway to the new time zone. This will also make jet lag easier for you and help your baby adjust when you return home.

Tip #3 Use daylight to adjust to a normal routine:

If you are a little further away, adjust to daylight as much as possible. It is a powerful stimulus for our body clock and everyone's sleep.

If you are flying east, use the light to wake your children naturally in the morning. It is best to leave the curtains open.

If you're flying west, use blackout blinds (there are also portable travel blinds) to block out the light and slumber a little longer. Hotel rooms usually have great blackout curtains.

You will probably be able to extend your children's waking time to adjust to the new time zone (with some fresh air and stimulus) but keep an eye on signs of tiredness and let them go to bed earlier if needed.

Tip #4 Adjust to the naptime and sleep schedule gradually:

It usually takes about a day for the body to adjust to each hour of time difference. Therefore, it may take a few days to properly adjust to the new time zone.

It tends to be easier to fly in the opposite direction, from east to west, as it's easier to stretch out a day (possibly with an extra power nap for the little ones) than to cut one short and go to bed at a decent bedtime before you're tired.

But honestly, just have fun. And if sleeping doesn't go to plan, a nap on the way to a beach in the pushchair or sling is better than no sleep at all. Stay relaxed and try to enjoy your holiday as much as possible.

CHAPTER 15

Looking After Yourself

Now, this may be a little controversial, but you HAVE to look after yourself first. Your baby relies on you, so prioritising thinking about you and keeping your head above water in the early days is paramount.

Looking after you IS looking after your baby.

Working on sleep is great for your baby, but also for you. If you sleep better, then you can feel rested. A well-rested parent is a happier, healthier parent.

Maintaining your physical and mental health and well-being is a priority. The well-meaning phrase of 'sleep when your baby sleeps' is full of good intentions but sometimes feels impossible. Accepting help can sometimes be hard when you'd prefer to do it your way.

Ten top tips for well-being

1. If always sleeping when the baby sleeps isn't feasible then just pick one nap, around lunchtime, to help break up the day and act as a little reset.

2. Temporarily have an earlier bedtime and go to bed with your baby. Your adult evenings will come back. If your sleep is very broken, then we can aim to maximise the overall sleep duration instead.

3. Use naps on the go to your advantage in the early days. They enable you to get outside and enjoy some fresh air and gentle exercise. You'll be flooded with a huge range of emotions in the early weeks (and beyond). Gentle exercise such as walking with your baby can help process these emotions.

4. Ask for help with specific tasks, whether that's from a partner, friend or extended family member. Be direct. For example, if they're popping over to see your new baby, ask them to pick up some milk or biscuits on their way.

5. Be realistic. This is a time of change, we ALL struggle with change. Forget the days of perfection. Aiming for 'good enough' is totally okay!

6. Remember what you eat affects how you feel. Try to aim for at least one healthy nutritious meal a day and supplement your diet if needed. There is an amazing range of home-delivered healthy services now if getting to the shops and cooking feels like too much.

7. You don't need to do ALL the things. A day at home and politely declining requests may just be what you need.

8. Treat yourself to the small things. Perhaps upgrade your shampoo or body wash so you really enjoy those five minutes! It's amazing how certain smells can have profound calming effects. Try products containing lavender or rose, they're known for their calming properties.

9. Stay hydrated. Have a water bottle, a big one! Just pop it next to you. You'll drink far more if it's in sight. The same goes for fruits and healthy snacks. Let those be the ones your body sees first!

10. Baby-wear to tick off the small stuff. There will be times when the jobs list seems endless and not all of us have access to 'a village'. A build-up of clutter and jobs can start to get on top of you. Baby-wearing is great for

tackling the list. Set aside 30 minutes each morning or afternoon to tick off some jobs. Be realistic, you don't have to do them all. Baby-wearing will let you be hands-free, and your little one will probably nap too. Once the clutter is cleared, it will help you feel more relaxed in your space for the rest of the day.

FURTHER SUPPORT

There are lots of additional resources available to support you with your little one's sleep.

Sign up for my Sleep Tips newsletter to get age-appropriate sleep support sent directly to your inbox.

Would you prefer personalised support? Contact me for a 15-minute sleep consultation to discuss the right support option for you.

www.childsleepspecialist.co.uk/contact

Follow me on Instagram @childsleepspecialist

SUPPORT DIRECTORY

Overall health and wellbeing

NHS (National Health Service)

- Comprehensive information on newborn care, including sleep, feeding, health, and development.
- www.nhs.uk/conditions/baby

NCT (National Childbirth Trust)

- A wide range of support for new and expectant parents, including classes, articles on baby care, and local support networks.
- www.nct.org.uk

NHS – Start4Life

- NHS-led advice on baby care, including sleep tips, breastfeeding, and weaning.
- www.nhs.uk/start4life

UNICEF UK Baby Friendly Initiative

- Guidance on breastfeeding and infant care, promoting best practices in health services.

- www.unicef.org.uk/babyfriendly/support-for-parents

Safe sleep

The Lullaby Trust

- Expert advice on safe sleep practices for babies, reducing the risk of sudden infant death syndrome (SIDS).
- www.lullabytrust.org.uk

Sleep

Child Sleep Specialist

- Expert advice and support on newborn sleep, tailored sleep plans, and resources for parents to establish healthy sleep foundations for their babies through childhood.
- www.childsleepspecialist.co.uk

Infant feeding

National Breastfeeding Helpline

- Free, confidential breastfeeding support from trained volunteers.
- www.nationalbreastfeedinghelpline.org.uk

La Leche League GB

- Support and information on breastfeeding, including guidance on weaning, mother-to-mother support groups, and a helpline for personalised advice.
- www.laleche.org.uk

First Steps Nutrition Trust

- Independent, evidence-based information on infant nutrition, including guides on weaning and healthy eating for babies.
- www.firststepsnutrition.org

Child Feeding Guide

- Evidence-based guidance on feeding children, including tips on introducing solids and managing fussy eating.
- www.childfeedingguide.co.uk

Twins & multiples

Twins Trust

- Support and resources for families with twins, triplets, and more, including guidance on sleep, feeding, weaning, and overall child care for multiples.
- www.twinstrust.org

Tiny babies and poorly babies

Tommy's

- Resources on pregnancy and baby care, with a focus on premature birth, stillbirth, and miscarriage support.
- www.tommys.org

Bliss

- Support for parents of babies born premature or sick, including guidance on sleep, feeding, and hospital care.
- www.bliss.org.uk

Cry-sis

- Support for families with excessively crying, sleepless, and demanding babies.
- www.cry-sis.org.uk

BIBILOGRAPHY

1. Yue W, Han X, Luo J, Zeng Z, Yang M. Effect of music therapy on preterm infants in neonatal intensive care unit: Systematic review and meta-analysis of randomized controlled trials. Journal of Advanced Nursing. 2021 Feb 17;77(2):635–52.

2. Bainbridge CM, Bertolo M, Youngers J, Atwood S, Yurdum L, Simson J, et al. Infants relax in response to unfamiliar foreign lullabies. Nature Human Behaviour. 2020 Oct 19;5(2):256–64.

3. Balk SJ, Bochner RE, Ramdhanie MA, Reilly BK, Bole A, Balk SJ, et al. Preventing Excessive Noise Exposure in Infants, Children, and Adolescents. Pediatrics. 2023 Nov 1;152(5).

4. Trust L. Rates of SIDS reach new record low but The Lullaby Trust warns against complacency. [Internet]. 2024 [cited 2024 Aug 13]. Available from: https://www.lullabytrust.org.uk/ons-2015/

5. Trust L. Safer sleep reduces the risk of SIDS. [Internet]. 2024 [cited 2024 Aug 13]. Available from: https://www.lullabytrust.org.uk/safer-sleep-advice/

6. NHS. Reduce the risk of sudden infant death syndrome (SIDS). [Internet]. 2021 [cited 2024 Aug 13]. Available from: https://www.nhs.uk/conditions/baby/caring-

for-a-newborn/reduce-the-risk-of-sudden-infant-death-syndrome/

7. Moon RY, Carlin RF, Hand I. Sleep-Related Infant Deaths: Updated 2022 Recommendations for Reducing Infant Deaths in the Sleep Environment. Pediatrics. 2022 Jul 1;150(1).

8. Schering S. AAP News. 2024 [cited 2024 Aug 13]. AAP leaders call decision to pull harmful weighted sleep products a "strong first step." Available from: https://publications.aap.org/aapnews/news/28768/AAP-leaders-call-decision-to-pull-harmful-weighted?autologincheck=redirected

9. Sexton S, Natale R. Risks and benefits of pacifiers. American family physician. 2009 Apr 15;79(8):681–5.

10. Paul IM, Hohman EE, Loken E, Savage JS, Anzman-Frasca S, Carper P, et al. Mother-Infant Room-Sharing and Sleep Outcomes in the INSIGHT Study. Pediatrics. 2017 Jul 1;140(1).

Printed in Great Britain
by Amazon

46330782R00056